# 60 SECOND time out

Published by
IntegrityWorks Coaching
14 Downing Street
Carlisle PA 17013
717-226-4306
www.integrityworkscoaching.com
mike@integrityworkscoaching.com



ISBN: 978-0-615-78588-2

Printed in the United States of America

***In memory of***
***Marilyn Joye Greene***
***May 1st, 1933 - May 10th, 2013***

***This book is dedicated*** to my inspiring wife, Amy, and our 3 fabulous children, Brittany, Madi and Mitchell.

***Thank you*** to all the wonderful people who made this book possible. First and most important I want to thank my wife for her inspiration and unconditional love, and her hours of listening, considering, and for her patience in editing my writing. She, as much as anyone, epitomizes the lessons in this book. Thank you to my brother, Jeff, for his unselfish dedication to the formatting and editing of this book, along with the creative and thought inspired cover design and graphics. Thank you also to my dear friend and long time mentor, Brett Deimler, whose uncharacteristic style and unending loyalty, inspired so many of these life lessons. It was Brett who taught our family the majority of these life lessons, by his example, his stories and his dedication. And a final thank you to my parents who have always set the ultimate example of loyalty, integrity and commitment.

# Table of Contents

*Most people don't need to be taught;*
*they just need to be reminded.*

- CS Lewis

# Lesson 1
# My Greatest Sale Ever

It was in 1990 that I made my greatest sale ever. The sales cycle in this case, was just over 2 years, and it's still technically in play to this very day.

This is something that goes back many, many years, when I first got into sales. I was new at the whole process, and did not really know much about it, at least not as much as I understood. When you really think about it, most people are selling all their lives. And as long as they are passionate about it, they are usually pretty good at it… that is, until they start thinking of it as selling. When they do, they move from passion to process. This is a change I'm so glad I never made in my greatest sale ever, and a lesson worth re-visiting often!

It is like trying to focus too much on your golf swing, your tennis swing, or whatever it is that you do – using the sports analogy. The more you think about it, the more you tend to mess it up! On the other hand, if you love it, and you're passionate about it, you commit, do what's right, stay in the game and let your desire and purpose lead your actions.

Let me get back to my greatest sale ever. In those early days, I was nervous about selling, and I was not very confident. I would compare myself to others and think, *Wow, how could I ever sell or accomplish the level of results that these people have? What a gap I have in terms of technique, skill and overall sales expertise!* Then my buddy, my good friend and mentor over many years, said this to me: "Mike, when you go home and you see your wife, you need to realize that she is your greatest sale ever and draw confidence from that." This was not meant in a stereotypical sales way, meaning I conned her into being my wife, but in a real perspective of sales - building the relationship, and building a foundation of trust and caring. When you think about the basic idea that people do business with people they know, like and trust (gotta be careful here!), you think about the reality of building the relationship. Good sales is not a one-night process. Good sales is a marriage. It is a long term process. Now, when it comes to marriage, I recommend one client (no, Amy's not a client – stay with me here!). In the true context of effective selling you want committed relationships with multiple clients - long term, deep, lasting relationships built on trust and caring.

So I look back and think, you know, she was and still is my greatest sale ever. This is not a sale I made once and then took for granted. This is a sale that I look to make every single day, and, thankfully, she does, too. She is, without question, my greatest sale ever and really where I still draw my greatest level of confidence in sales and in life.

*Choose the work you love, and you'll never have to work a day in your life.*

- Confuscious

# Lesson 2
# When Life Works List

What are your "Best Practices"?

Do you know what you were doing when life worked best this year?

I heard an interview with Sean Stevenson, author of *Get Off Your Butt*, within which he offered an idea I highly endorse. He spoke of creating a "WLWL" - as he calls, a "When Life Works List". What key actions or habits did you engage in when life seemed to be working best? This can be applied to life as a whole or a specific key part. We are happiest and thereby, most productive, when we are pleased with our actions. This is a great exercise for any individual or team strategic planning process.

Fall is my favorite season of all! I love the cool, crisp air, the color of the leaves and the promise of clean, white snow (the first snow is always the best!).

Fall is also planning time for me personally and professionally. This is the time I usually take a day or two to slow down, think, reflect and begin to develop plans for the upcoming year. What worked for me this year and why? What was going on when life worked best for me? What do I want to accomplish – personally and professionally – in the coming year? This starts with identifying the "big rocks", then creating annual outcomes for each area – some will be more tangible than others, but I don't sweat it too much. It's most important to just get started toward something that will demonstrate progress in each specific "big rock".

This typically results in an overhauled "life plan" and a revised business/sales plan each year. My ultimate goal is to be measurably better in the key areas of my life at the end of each year. I know I cannot improve what I don't measure, and it's hard to measure what I don't map. Mapping is the strategy.

If you are responsible for results – whether on your job, in your business, in your home, at your church, or simply for personal improvement and you have not set your plan for the coming year, I encourage you to block out time to work through it.

A good plan, executed, measured and adjusted accordingly can be extremely rewarding.

Think about it right now…if you are not pleased with your growth in the things that matter most to you, do you have a map to measure it and to show why?

Time to get one!

*The single biggest problem in communication is the illusion that it has taken place.*

- George Bernard Shaw

# Lesson 3
# Becoming Stupid

Ever say something you regretted immediately after you said it? Picture this – you're heading home, late again and knowing a fight is about to ensue. You walk through the door and immediately feel the tension. As you approach your spouse, your blood pressure is up, your heart begins to race a bit, and you feel a little flush. The ensuing conversation is all too predictable and leaves you feeling lousy, saying things you didn't mean. You were focused completely on a strong defense and sought to win the inevitable argument, when in actuality you forgot you are both on the same team! How about a mistake at work, poor performance on the job or a client's call after a less than stellar performance? What's that conversation like? Any regretful words or emotions? Again, aren't we on the same team? Why the defense? Why the antagonistic feelings? Why not intelligently work through the issue to a mutually rewarding conclusion?

Why is it that when things get heated and emotions run strong –whether at home, with a client, with a peer, or just out in the community – we seem to lose some level of sanity and certainly some level of intelligence? Now, some have mastered this challenge – either naturally or through learned behavior. Most of us, however, aren't even aware of what is happening, when it is happening, until it's too late.

Fact is when we step into a conversation where opinions differ and emotions run strong, we really do become stupid, or at least less intelligent. Referenced in a book called *Crucial Conversations*, I read about a study that shows exactly what is going on in our bodies, physiologically, in these heated moments.

Have you ever heard of "fight or flight"? That's the body's natural response to a potentially dangerous situation. Whether it's physical or not, doesn't matter; our response is the same – we experience redirected blood and oxygen flow to the extremities best suited for fight or flight – muscles! Unfortunately, the most important part of our body, our brain, becomes somewhat starved in the process. Yes, that's right - we feed our muscles and starve our brain. And you know what less blood and oxygen to the brain means? Stupidity! And we've all experienced it.

How do we overcome this? Very carefully, for sure, and it's much too involved for this short article. But I can offer two simple ideas from the book, *Crucial Conversations*. First, maintain mutual respect. It's difficult for respect not to be reciprocal. Attacking is not respectful. You get the idea. Second, maintain mutual purpose. Keep the real issue in sight, not defending your position and attacking theirs, but to accomplish the purpose you both have – the one that is bigger than the moment.

Always make the relationship more important than the situation. That will keep everyone safe!

*"Although it's admirable to be ambitious and hard-working, it's more desirable to be smart-working."*

- John Maxwell

# Lesson 4
# Purposeful Time Blocking

One key to success is a simple but powerful technique called "time blocking." Time blocking involves consistently setting aside time for the high priority activities – those that are important (urgent or not) as it relates to the critical growth areas in your life. When you use time blocking you are, in essence, making an appointment with yourself! Ideally you should block time for important activities in both your work and personal life that will have the greatest impact on the growth you desire.

**Personal Time Blocking -**
You cannot be effective in your work if your inner reserves are depleted. Making time to "recharge your batteries" will actually boost your energy. Block time for exercise, contemplation, relaxation or recreation. Be sure to carve out time for family or friends as well. And, before committing to anything else, be sure to pencil in some vacation time, too – this is very important! Then, treat appointments with yourself as respectfully as you would with others.

**Time Blocking at Work -**
What if you had two uninterrupted hours every day to focus on nothing else but your most important activities? The time might be spent planning or working on one or more projects, sales calls or marketing efforts, personal development, networking, or learning something that will add value to your work. Just two hours dedicated to the really important things. Keep in mind that these two hours are focused, uninterrupted work time and do not include all the other time spent traveling, in meetings, talking by phone, sending emails or any other activities not directly related to your original focus.

As a salesperson and/or business owner, consider the major things you might want to schedule into personal appointments (time blocked) in order to plan and execute for optimal effectiveness. For example, when I started in print sales, it became clear that face to face appointments were critical to developing relationships that would grow into significant clients. I decided one of the most important activities I was neglecting was the one that would usually yield the most appointments – phone calls to schedule those appointments! This was one of my least preferred sales activities, yet I knew if I just planned the calls and followed through, I would get results. And that I did. Each morning around 8:30 I had a personal appointment with myself to make calls. This time was treated at the same level of importance as a typical sales appointment – meaning I would not see other people, take other calls, check email, or do anything other than remain focused on the purpose of my appointment during this time. You can even take this a step further and tell your manager or an accountability partner that you have these "personal appointments" – creating a level of accountability.

The bottom line as it relates to sales: clarify the goals you most want to accomplish this year and the key tasks respective to your success; then schedule personal appointments with yourself (recurring or planned) to execute the tasks you've identified.

Make personal appointments with yourself to achieve the success you want!

*The future will depend on what we do in the present.*
- Mahatma Ghandi

# Lesson 5
# The Journey Is The Destination

During an unprecedented October snowfall, our kids headed out to play in the snow, and my wife suggested we go out and join them. We tossed on our snow clothes and headed out to meet our kids, including our yellow Lab, who thinks she is a kid, too. We headed to the golf course hills and found the group fighting for speed in the wet, slow snow. Mitchell decided we needed to build a ramp to jump start our sled run, so we invested the next hour working with easy-packing snow building this enormous ramp. It was a great start for the slow run. Ironically, once we built it, we took three or four runs and decided we were all cold and wet – time to head home.

Isn't that often the case? We invest so much time in the journey in order to get to the destination, only to find the journey was the real destination. We had more fun building the ramp than we did using what we built. Strangely, our family often enjoys the car ride to our vacation destination almost as much as the vacation itself. In sales, I learned to CHOOSE to enjoy the difficult activities that led to the rewarding results. It was in those activities I grew the most, and I figured if I had to invest my time and life anyway in making calls, setting appointments, presenting ideas and solutions, I might as well CHOOSE to enjoy all of it. Enjoying the moments made them better for those I was around as well, and ultimately helped me succeed.

Life is too precious not to enjoy the moments between the rewards. Let's make a conscious decision to enjoy the minutes, hours and days that lead up to whatever we think we are after, making the most of every day we are gifted. A mentor of mine always reminded me to ENJOY THE JOURNEY. He was and is absolutely right.

Helen Keller said, "Is life not a thousand times too short to bore ourselves"?

*The harder you work, the harder it is to surrender.*

- Vince Lombardi

# Lesson 6

# A Dog In The Hunt Don't Know He Has Fleas!

There's a story of two boys standing on one side of a freshly snow covered field. The one boy challenged the other that he could run a straighter path across the field than the other. Both agreed and the first boy took off. As he went, he would occasionally look down and back to check his pattern while he ran. Once there, he looked back only to see a very crooked, jagged line across the field. The second boy picked a visual target across the field, fixed his eyes and took off. As he ran, his focus never left its visual target until he made it to the other side. You know the result – a very direct, straight path!

Have you ever left your office to go do something seemingly important, only to be distracted by something (phone, email, kids, co-workers, magazine article, newspaper, TV, a bug!) along the way? Then, after several MORE distractions, you finally arrive back at your desk only to find you never did what you originally set out to do!

So what's your target? What or who NEEDS your undivided attention?

- Dinner with your spouse
- Meeting with a client
- An important conversation with an employee
- Playing a game with your daughter
- Reading a devotion

Sometimes we need to ignore the cell phone, texts, and email notifications, close the door, tell others we're not to be disturbed, show some assertiveness, say "no", turn off the TV, fold up the paper and control our ever straying thoughts.

Fix your focus on what is important at this moment – planned or not - and the distractions will be less visible, less appealing and less destructive. Be absent in anything but the moment, keep your focus and as scripture says, "Press toward the mark of the prize…"

Be in the hunt when and with whom it matters, and remember, a dog in the hunt don't know he has fleas!

*It isn't what you have or who you are or where you are or what you are doing that makes you happy or unhappy. It is what you think about it.*

- Dale Carnegie

# Lesson 7
# The Little Man

Some time ago I was walking past my laptop and noticed a consistent forming and reforming of 3 dimensional pipes on the screen. The screen saver was doing what it was programmed to do when not in use. Of course, once I sat down and went to work, it snapped right to attention. Isn't that just how our brain works? We are always thinking, whether we're aware of it or not. And what may be really scary is what we are thinking when we are not thinking - our mental screen saver. I believe that what is on that screen saver is the key to where we are really headed, the future we have yet to realize. Are we not thinking about what we don't want, don't have, or fear? Are we not thinking about a recent argument with our spouse, or one we think we'll have in the next few minutes? Are we not thinking about the poor sales we're experiencing, the money we don't have, the shape we're not in, the promises and commitments we haven't kept? Remember, even when we're not thinking we are thinking - potentially hours upon hours each day!

Years ago we taught our kids why and how to guard their gates - mostly their eyes and ears. But this advice isn't just for kids - it's for all of us who care where we are going. Decide to filter what influences your thoughts, and thereby your screen saver. Just as background music at a department store can set the music in our minds much of the day, our environment - aware of it or not - is always influencing what makes up our screen saver.

I remember hearing Earl Nightingale's classic recording from the 1950's, *The Strangest Secret.* He spoke of a great earth machine, with all its size, power and influence - being led by a tiny little man sitting way up on top. The machine really doesn't care; it just does what it is directed to do. This year, be ever more deliberate about engaging that little man - to get that screen saver working for you.

*Losers focus on what they are going through;*
*winners focus on what they are going to.*
- John Maxwell

# Lesson 8
# The Twig Of '93

Trained professional: "We are going around the leaf." Ant in procession: "Around the leaf? I don't think we can do that." Trained professional: "Oh, nonsense, this is nothing compared to the twig of '93."

Are you familiar with this classic lesson from one of life's greatest teachers, Pixar? It came out of the first 2 minutes and 44 seconds of "A Bug's Life", and it speaks volumes about today's society. Much like the ants that are walking in procession, only to have one suddenly interrupted by a leaf falling in its direct path, many people today are often paralyzed by seemingly small challenges in their day.

I believe the point of the Pixar writers, and definitely the one I am trying to make here, is that leaves fall all the time, unplanned, untimely; yet to get on with our lives, looking at the leaf won't move us forward. We need a mentality that focuses on getting past that leaf – around it, over it, under it, or even through it. Unfortunately, most people are problem spotters, rather than problem solvers.

Over the years my wife and I have drilled this concept into our kids. When a challenge arises, we simple say,

"Go around the leaf." Or another mantra from a very wise friend of ours, "problems are meant to be solved, not lived with" – love that perspective and attitude!

What stops you in your tracks? What small blips completely derail your masterful plan for the day? Did you get a flat tire? Did the prospect cancel? Did that huge order fall through? Did you oversleep this morning? Did you twist your ankle playing basketball? A few clicks with Google and you'll find remarkable examples of people who not only overcame major challenges, but learned to thrive in the solutions. And honestly, in most of my cases, the challenges are truly leaves – little blips along my path.

Bottom line: You can choose to be a problem spotter or problem solver.

*The purpose of our lives is to add value to the people of this generation and those that follow.*

- Buckminster Fuller

# Lesson 9
# Choosing High Energy

Have you ever met someone who just "was someone" when they walked in the room? They didn't necessarily do anything unusual or special, but for some intuitive reason, you just knew they were "somebody", and so did everyone else. Now, we are all "somebody", but few of us view ourselves that way. I don't mean in an arrogant, self-serving sort of way; but rather, a way that suggests inner confidence and ultimate self-assuredness. I can think of a few people who fit this description and one thing that seems to be apparent in all of these people is ENERGY or PRESENCE. They exude energy, purpose, direction. I remember reading in David Schwartz's book, *The Magic of Thinking Big*, that to gain confidence, we should consciously walk 25% faster – because it looks as if we KNOW where we are going and we're excited to get there (why wouldn't we be , if we, being confident and purposeful, chose to go there in the first place?!). I believe we can increase our physical energy through good habits like eating, rest and exercise. But we can also create good energy (presence) through choice - simply by being purpose-driven in all we do – not necessarily goal driven, purpose-driven.

Next time you're at an event – business or pleasure, doesn't matter, look around and see if you can spot that person of unique presence. Take a "chance" and introduce yourself – you might be surprised how much can be learned in that moment. Perhaps at some point, if not already, you'll be that person for someone else.

*The greatest victory is over self.*

- Aristotle

# Lesson 10
# Painful Enough For Change?

A story I heard years ago goes something like this…

A man walks into an old general store to pick up a few things. As he is walking around he occasionally hears this low groaning sound. As he approaches the counter, he sees the sound is coming from an old dog lying beside the counter. He asks the owner what's wrong with the dog, and the owner says, "Oh, that's old Rex, and that's just his spot. He's been lying there for years, and over time a nail has worn part way through the floor board. The nail is jagging him as he lays there, and he's constantly groaning about it". The man asks the obvious question, "Why doesn't he just move to another spot?" The owner casually gives the same answer most of us could give, "Well, it does hurt him, but apparently not enough to do anything about it."

Can we relate? What changes do we want to make, need to make, that we are not making because not changing doesn't hurt enough? The bigger question might be, when it does hurt enough, is it too late? A buddy of mine always used to say, "Bloom where you are planted." So if we plant ourselves, by choice, in a place that causes some pain, yet we don't change, then bloom there. Or commit to change.

How do we make these changes? One way is to visualize the future we'll have without making the changes. If you're a salesperson and you don't make the calls, eventually the pipeline will dry up – and so will the bank account. If you are a business owner and you don't work on your business, you may find yourself way down the wrong road. If you're a husband and you don't plan time with your wife and your kids, you'll miss out on the things that matter most and set a poor example for that next generation. This honest visualization paints a vivid reality that may make the pain of change hurt LESS than the pain of staying the same.

Another way is to ask someone to hold you accountable to the change you know you need. Find someone you trust and respect, and who will follow through on the tough job of accountability. Tell them the change you will make and create a system of accountability with them. I've sometimes done this with my kids – hard to carve out a creative excuse with my kids, knowing it's also teaching them how to live.

Accountability can be especially powerful. Sometimes that person can help you find the nail you didn't know was there.

*Nothing so conclusively proves a man's ability to lead others, as what he does from day to day to lead himself.*

- Tom Watson

# Lesson 11
# Lead Positive Personal Change

One thing is for sure, and you know it before you read it: change is inevitable; growth is optional. So don't be a victim of the changes around you; be the victor of change within you.

If you could back up one year and then look ahead to where you are now –would you have written your goals (both business/professional and personal) at that time to match the results you have now? The answers for all the change we desire in our lives are all around us – in books, in people, in articles, on the internet (just Google it!); so with the plethora of knowledge, why are most of us in the same place today as we were a year ago, or worse – further behind? There can be many reasons, but let me identify one major reason: lack of accountability.

As a business owner and former commissioned sales professional, I encourage you to stop working in your business (sales development) and start working *on* your business! For example, make a list of what you think a highly successful sales professional should be doing to develop and improve their success. What would a successful year look like and how would you reward yourself? What are your key performance measures – how much in sales do you need to produce just to meet your goal – this year, this month, this week, today? What are the corresponding activity goals that will yield these results? Do you know your average sale amount, your hit ratios (closing percentages), and your ideal client profile? Do you have an annual sales plan that would convince a banker to bet on you? What routines can be systemized in your sales system to develop predictability, consistency and accuracy of priorities and related activities? Do you test and measure to find out what works and what doesn't? How about the personal side – your family, your marriage, your finances, your health, your spiritual growth? Are they any better than last year at this time? Is there room for improvement?

These are just some of the areas of consideration in leading change both professionally and personally. Now this is just a quick look, but it sure gets things going in the right direction – and as Robert Shuller says, "Beginning is half done"!

So how does accountability fit in? As I said, all of what is written above is readily available at the local bookstore or online. Knowledge is only part of the challenge; the rest is application. Though incredibly influential and valuable, books, CDs, DVDs, websites, and magazines – none of these make good counselors, mentors or coaches. They cannot speak to the uniqueness of the individual. Only a person can do that – particularly one you respect and trust, yet outside the "box" of your business and personal life.

Find someone who is qualified, purposeful, and dedicated to your success and request his or her help! None of us is as good as all of us!

*People often say that motivation doesn't last. Well, neither does bathing - that's why we recommend it daily.*

- Zig Ziglar

# Lesson 12
# Remember To Sharpen Your Axe

A young man approached the foreman of a logging crew and asked for a job.

"That depends," replied the foreman. "Let's see you fell this tree." The young man stepped forward and skillfully felled a great tree. Impressed, the foreman exclaimed, "You can start Monday."

Monday, Tuesday, Wednesday, Thursday rolled by. Thursday afternoon the foreman approached the young man and said, "You can pick up your paycheck on the way out today."

Startled, the young man replied, "I thought you paid on Friday."

"Normally we do," said the foreman. "But we're letting you go today because you've fallen behind. Our daily felling charts show that you've dropped from first place on Monday to last place today."

"But I'm a hard worker," the young man objected. "I arrive first, leave last and even have worked through my coffee breaks!"

The foreman, sensing the young man's integrity, thought for a minute and then asked, "Have you been sharpening your axe?"

The young man replied, "No, sir, I've been working too hard to take time for that!"

How do you sharpen your axe? Think of what and who can sharpen your axe – mentors, books, CD's and DVD's, your spouse, family, prayer, and even exercise.

When do you sharpen your axe? What routine is needed to get the most of your efforts? Build the habit of routine sharpening in order to make your efforts as effective as possible.

*You affect your conscious mind by verbal repetition.*
- W Clement Stone

# Lesson 13
# Power In Your Words

A mentor once told me that the word "can't" means "won't". What? He meant that I should empower myself through my words, rather than so often doing just the opposite. Words mean things and, whether we like it or not, the words we choose either empower or disarm us. Have you ever said you can't do something – call someone, meet someone, be somewhere, accomplish something? Is that really true - or can you, but you choose not to - either by finding something more important to do or by negatively choosing to believe you can't. It's a matter of honesty, choice and responsibility.

I remember my son (4 or 5 at the time) leaving his sled at the bottom of a small hill by our home. I told him to bring it in, and he said "I can't". A learning opportunity – I told him "can't means won't", and he promptly said "alright then, I won't!" Now, that was funny, true and led to another lesson!

Bottom line: let's own the words we choose and the actions they imply; otherwise, words like "can't" will subconsciously teach us that we are not in control. To be sure, there will certainly be times when "can't" really does apply, but I suspect it is far less than we think. Remember, we are the sum total of the circumstances we've encountered and the choices we have made.

*Whatever the mind of a man can conceive and believe, it can achieve. Thoughts are things! Strong, deeply rooted desire is the starting point of all achievement.*

- Napoleon Hill

# Lesson 14
# Thinking For A Change

If I can get you to think through this brief summary, it will have been a successful endeavor! Henry Ford said, "Thinking is the hardest work there is, which is the probable reason why so few engage in it." John Maxwell wrote an entire book called, T*hinking for a Change*. Michael Gerber, in his bestselling book, T*he E-Myth* says that most business owners are too busy working "in" their business; they rarely take time to work "on" their business. Thinking! The top selling book of all time, *The Bible*, in Philippians says, "Finally, brothers, whatever is true, whatever is noble, whatever is right, whatever is pure, whatever is lovely, whatever is admirable--if anything is excellent or praiseworthy--think about such things."

One of many challenges associated with deliberate thinking time is the presence of silence. A friend and mentor often told me that most people are terrified of silence. They will fill the silence, and hence their mind, with something - music, talk radio, TV, or even "white noise". I am not judging any of this, but only suggesting that perhaps there is unique value in simply taking time to literally slow down and think.

Perhaps you can leverage something you already do or simply recognize the value it offers in applying this idea. Let's be honest, many of us get our greatest ideas in the shower! Others, like me, find great thinking time while exercising – assuming the distractions are eliminated. Personally, running represents one of the most valuable times in my day – not just for the physical benefit, but for the mental benefit. Thinking while running (no iPod, music, etc – just me and the outside world) comes without effort and provides a level of clarity, focus and creativity I rarely experience any other time of the day.

Think about the day; think about what you appreciate; think about how to do a task; think about how to serve a client; think about what to do with your family this weekend; think about how to improve your company, your job, your church, your community; think about how to become a better person; think about what is good. Or perhaps we can take time to occasionally think about "nothing" – thereby listening – to surfacing subconscious thoughts, listening to an answer to prayer, or just listening (and appreciating) the sounds around us.

Let's exercise the most powerful creation ever known – our mind. THINK ABOUT IT and prosper!

*Ninety percent of those who fail are not actually defeated. They simply quit.*

\- Paul J Meyer

# Lesson 15
# Action Cures Fear

Fear knocked at the door; Faith answered, and no one was there.

Much like the idea that you cannot have two dominant thoughts at the same time, when you act, fear is suppressed. It may still be there; but it isn't dominant, because we are in a different mode – we're in action.

So why don't you take action? What are you fearful of?

*Reactions of others…*

*Perceived failure…*

*Responsibility…*

*Rejection…*

*Judgment or criticism…*

*Disappointment…*

Think about the time you asked your wife out on that first date, or your first job interview, or that first sales call, or your first public speech. While you may have experienced fear while you took action, most of the fear was experienced just before you acted. Once you began the conversation, the interview or that first sales call, your action suppressed the fear. The more you kept in the action mode, the less fear you experienced.

Most of the fear I experience in life happens in advance of what I fear - it's my sick form of preparation. I remember hearing a point made by Dennis Waitley that said something like this: People tend to replay past failure (hence the sense of fear and worry) rather than pre-play future success. This fear generally inspires a habit of doubt. And doubt can be a paralyzing thing in our lives. Mark Twain said, "Our doubts are traitors that make us lose the good we might oft win by fearing to attempt." We become paralyzed and the thing we fear, though it hasn't actually happened, leads us to miss out on what we could and should have gained through meaningful action!

Perhaps there is something to the Nike slogan, "Just Do It!" At least if it falls within the ethics of good choices and your own personal and professional filters, and you've somewhat adhered to the "5 P's" (Proper Preparation Prevents Poor Performance) – I like it! "Just Do It!"

Clarify what you want and the fears that hold you back. Commit to overcome them with action. Commit to someone else you respect. Create rewards for action and possibly consequences for inaction. Begin to build healthy pride in overcoming fear.

If it's morally right, poses opportunity for growth in areas that really matter to you, then take it from Nike - Just Do It!

*What lies behind us and what lies ahead of us pales in comparison to what lies within us.*

- Henry David Thoreau

# Lesson 16
# Capacity Is A State Of Mind

Why is one person making $50,000 a year and another making $5million a year? Is it that the second one is super duper productive or just incredibly lucky? Certainly talent, skill, experience, discipline, etc., plays into the picture – but to the tune of 10,000% difference? Doubt it. Perhaps one's perception of capacity is very different from the other. Imagine that, their mind's perception of what each can achieve is different. Very different. I've read that sales people generally "see" themselves at a certain income/revenue level and when they begin to exceed that level, they'll often subconsciously sabotage their results and end up right where they "think" they belong – much too their disappointment.

Change our beliefs and we'll begin to change our results. Remember, we tend not to get what we want, but what we expect. This expectation (capacity) is determined by our chosen state of mind. Change it by changing your input – associate with bigger thinkers through people, books, podcasts, magazines, and your self talk and imagination. Dennis Waitley says to stop REplaying past failures and start PREplaying future success. Say it, see it, expect it, got it!

*Poor people have a big TV. Rich people have a big library.*
- Jim Rohn

# Lesson 17
# Pigs Don't Know Pigs Stink!

A few days ago my wife mentioned this phrase that a wise friend of ours used to say: "Pigs don't know pigs stink." Wow! There is so much truth and learning in this one little statement, I had to write about it! And just so we're clear, in the context of my wife's comment, I'm pretty sure I was not the pig.

Regardless, the fact of the matter is true, and pigs really don't know it – they stink! My buddy would say this often when referencing negative people. His point was simple: if we are negative and hang out with negativity, we don't know the difference. This applies across the board. If I am in sales and in the bottom 20%, but hang out with the bottom 20%, I really don't know it. If I am constantly bashing my wife with my friends, and they do the same, none of us knows the difference. In either case, we are feeding each other by always relating – unfortunately in a negative way! That is not to say we don't really know the difference; it's just that our environment does not support an awareness to positively change. So we just keep on slopping along in the mud!

One of the most valuable life lessons I learned was nearly 20 years ago – and yes, it was from that same friend. He taught me the value of positive association, specifically through reading a little every day from something that would inspire positive change in me. Books about leadership, people skills, communication, marriage, kids and parenting, finances, sales, etc., became a consistent element of daily association. After about 30 days I began to notice that many people around me were more and more negative. What was really happening is that I was changing and noticing the difference. They were not more negative; I was more positive.

Keeping with the theme, the pig (me) cleaned up and began to notice the mud, dirt, slime, etc that was around me (not the people, the attitudes and perspective!).

What about you? Are your sales where you want them? If not, check the sty – is it full of sales people at your level and below? If your marriage is not the way you want it, check the sty – is it full of people who relate and even seem to thrive on similar issues, without ever solving them? If you don't like your health, check the sty – is it full of others who constantly struggle with weight, exercise, and general fitness? If we want to change anything, let's check the sty and find the people who reflect the change we want in ourselves.

*You'll be the same five years from now as you are today except for the people you meet and the books that you read.*

- Charlie "Tremendous" Jones

## Lesson 18
# How Do You View Life?

I remember hearing a story that goes something like this: A grandfather was sleeping on a couch one day when his grandson decided to play a joke on him. He went to the refrigerator and pulled out some limburger cheese, extra smelly. He went over to his sleeping grandfather and gently rubbed a little of the cheese on his mustache. Hiding around the corner, he noticed his grandfather twitching and finally waking up. He bolted upright, took a deep sniff and said, "Something in here stinks!" He immediately got up and moved into the kitchen, took another deep breath and again said, "It stinks in here, too!" Looking for some relief, he went outside, took one more deep breath, and finally said, "The whole world stinks!"

Of course grandpa will eventually determine the real source of the stink and quickly get rid of it with a little soap and water, making things seem sweet once again. Anyone with this foul stuff on the inside, however, has a much more difficult task.

In his book, *Winning With People*, John Maxwell says that

we all have a personal frame of reference that consists of our attitudes, assumptions, and expectations concerning ourselves, other people, and life. He states that these factors determine whether we're optimistic or pessimistic, cheerful or gloomy, trusting or suspicious, friendly or reserved, brave or timid. These factors tend to color how we view life. Ultimately the only way to change the way we view life is to change ourselves from the inside out.

This is no easy task and certainly not a one shot deal. Change in attitude can be relatively easy in the moment, but very difficult (though simple) in the habit. This change is best accomplished the way it started– through small, consistent, daily decisions and influences. The simplest answer, in my humble opinion, is found in Charlie "Tremendous" Jones' famous statement, "You'll be the same in five years as you are today, except for the people you meet and the books that you read."

So who are you associating with most frequently and consistently – in terms of people and books? Does their view of life and overall attitude reflect the change you want? This question is the answer.

*Success is walking from failure to failure with no loss of enthusiasm.*

\- Winston Churchill

# Lesson 19
# The Latte Principle

As of this moment, a tall latte at Starbuck's sells for $3, according ASK.com. Buy one every day (two if you are a couple), five days a week, and that's $30 per week or $1,560 per year. At a tax rate of 25%, you'd have to make over $2,000 to keep enough to cover the annual tall latte investment plan! Vacation anyone?

But really, who thinks in terms of the annual impact of what would appear to be a $3 decision? Truly, most of us only think in isolation – a $3 latte, a negative thought, or a temporary moment of distraction of our time to visit Foxsports.com. One peak at the landing page – which usually bleeds into 10, 15, or even 20 minutes – a couple times a day, could actually be upwards of an hour and a half a week, or 78 hours a year! Funny, this is my home page!

Or perhaps most devastating - our thoughts... Imagine if God decided to produce an annual report of our recurring thoughts ranked in order of appearance. What would the most common thoughts be? How often would they show up, and what cumulative impact do they have? I suspect if

I saw that report on me, I would be far more proactive at filtering and purposefully leading what I think.

Whether it's about our finances, our time, or our thoughts, I believe that if we would immediately see the long term impact of our decisions in these matters, we would make impulse and, ultimately, habitual decisions very differently. I believe we would edit our thoughts more carefully, choose our expenditures more wisely, and ultimately be more proactive with how and with whom we invest our time.

Just curious, anyone reading this while enjoying a tall latte at your local Starbuck's? It's all good!

*Most of your unhappiness in life is due to the fact that you are listening to yourself rather than talking to yourself.*

- D Martin Lloyd-Jones

# Lesson 20
# True Colors

What's in your head? Right now – what are you singing, thinking, feeling? Why?

The other day we were sitting at the dinner table, and I suddenly blurt out, "Why do I have Cyndi Lauper's "True Colors" stuck in my mind?" This is not a common song for me, and I didn't remember anyone in my house singing it out loud…Then, just as I finished asking the question, my wife and I both looked on the counter at her recent library book selection, *True Colors*. The book and the song are unrelated, and as I thought a little more, I realized that when I came home, I simply noticed the book. Nothing more. No questions about it. My wife didn't even see me seeing it. I just walked by, noticed it and continued on. An hour or two later we were finishing dinner when I asked the question about the song in my head.

Wow! How powerful our mind is! I never even consciously recognized the song or related it from the book title, but some guy in my subconscious made the connection between the book title and ordered the song for my background listening pleasure. Unfortunately, my lyric memory is highly limited as I generally end up repeating one line of the songs chosen by this guy – over and over again, often for hours!

Why do I bring this up? Remember the saying, "See no evil, hear no evil, speak no evil"? Whatever we see, hear, feel, experience – regardless of our conscious awareness – goes in our mind and influences our thinking, which eventually influences our actions and thereby our results.

So, if you don't have what you want in the big rocks of your life – your career, your marriage, your health, etc., ask this critical question: "Is what I am exposed to – what I see, what I hear (this includes what I say out load (speaking into existence)) reflective of what I want or what I have?" Really think on this. What a difference it can really make!

"…I see your true colors, shining through; I see your true colors, and that's why…"

Enjoy your music selection!

*Just as your car runs more smoothly and requires less energy to go faster and farther when the wheels are in perfect alignment, you perform better when your thoughts, feelings, emotions, goals and values are in balance.*

- Brian Tracy

# Lesson 21
# Success Is A Balance

J Paul Getty was, by most people's standards, super financially successful; but relationally –well, married beyond 5 times by most people's standards is not success. Balance is the issue. As we progress in our profession, how much balance do we have in our marriage, our family, and our relationships? What about spiritual development and physical health? I learned (and continue re-learning) that success is a balance – of those four key pillars: spiritual, financial, physical, and relational. By my standard, I am not a success if I achieve remarkable financial gain at the expense of my family, my health, or my soul. And I don't believe one takes from the other – we can have financial success while building a loving family, lasting friendships, good health, and spiritual growth. Consider also that balance offers security – when one pillar falls, three others hold us up.

Today's economic change and uncertainty has resulted in difficult financial setbacks for countless people – how much better off are those who have their faith and family to support and lead them back on track? Take the necessary time and energy to identify and apply value filters that will eliminate growth in one area at the expense of another – thereby always growing in BALANCE.

*If you don't design your own plan, chances are you'll fall into someone else's plan. And guess what they have planned for you? Not much.*

- Jim Rohn

# Lesson 22
# A Clear Vision Makes For Easy Decisions

I heard a speaker many years ago say, "When vision is clear, decisions are easy". I'm no pilot, but I suspect a clear day makes for much easier and quicker decisions than a cloudy day (all other things equal) - because you can see your pathway and perhaps your destination. The simple fact is that when we know exactly what we are striving for, the decisions around us are much easier to make because they have bearing on something concrete and decidedly important. For example, if my vision is to honor my wife, stopping at a bar with a female co-worker is an easy decision (that would be a "no"). If I am training for a marathon, deciding whether or not to run today is easy. If I want people to trust me, following through on a promise is an easy decision. Once you know exactly where you want to go, choose to make decisions that will move you closer to that goal, rather than decisions that will lead you further from it. Knowing the vision/goal, then understanding the impact of each decision makes this process so much simpler. And, be aware - indecision is a decision not to decide; otherwise a "no" until further notice. For that reason, we are all making daily decisions – the question is whether or not they are leading us where we want to go. So, yes – when vision is clear, decisions are easy!

*Efficiency is doing things right;*
*effectiveness is doing right things.*
- Peter Drucker

# Lesson 23
# Building Constraints

I remember hearing that in order to be on top in sales you need to work 80+ hours a week – at least for the first few years. Don't believe it! The effort needed to accomplish a task will expand to fit the time it is given. And if no constraint is provided, it will overflow like a flood. Immediately I placed constraints on my sales time, and when I did hit #1, I was "working" less than 40 hours a week.

Do you believe in the power of constraints? Do you set and abide by them? There are always extenuating circumstances – the challenge is keeping them from becoming the norm. Incidentally, this concept need not be limited to work. Have you ever heard the phrase "they're so heavenly bound, they're no earthly good"? Faith is important to me, so don't read what I am not saying. But it does not keep me from living - dating my wife, serving my clients, loving my kids, staying fit – truly I believe faith enhances all those interactions.

One mentor said to me, "Show me your calendar, and I'll show you your priorities." Now, I don't put my kids in my calendar (formally), but I do constrain my working hours, and we do protect family dinners, date night and family night (in our home every night is family night, unless it's date night). My way is the right way for me, not necessarily the next person; but it is important to understand that if I was not deliberate in constraining my work, family and date nights would exist sporadically, at best.  And for our family, that would not be good.

Constraints are a natural phenomenon – oceans, lakes, and rivers – all constrained; yet when released, disaster occurs.

I am convinced that constraints bring value, focus and purpose to what we hold to be important in our lives. Yet, it takes a decision and disciplined follow through, and often a lot of faith, to honor the constraints we know we need.

*In matters of style, swim with the current; in matters of principle, stand like a rock.*

- Thomas Jefferson

# Lesson 24
# Honor Your Big Rocks

Many of you have heard the story author Stephen Covey related in his book, *The Seven Habits of Highly Effective People*, about the big rocks. Paraphrased a bit, it is about a professor presenting an empty jug to his class. Holding it up, he claims it to be empty, then fills it with big rocks. He asks the class if it is full and gets an affirmative response from most. He then proceeds to add small stones, then sand, then water – finally filling it completely. The point, he states, is that you could not get the big rocks in if they were not put in first.

Okay, great story. Wow. I should think about this. Wait, what is that email? Who is calling? What's on TV tonight? What's tomorrow's weather? Wonder what the baseball score is. On and on, the distractions dilute the potential life changing impact of this important lesson. Stop. Focus.

What are the big rocks – what matters most? If you own a business (consider your professional career a "business"), step out of that box and look from a 5, 10 and even 20 year perspective. Looking back over your career from that far out –ask yourself what mattered most? Go ahead… What made the biggest difference or would have? If you're really ambitious, try this from a life perspective… and start writing.

Once you have your big rocks – plug them into your schedule first; and if that is not feasible, be sure to default or "time block" (an appointment with yourself) to act on them in some planned fashion.

Honor the Big Rocks!

*The loudest and most influential voice you hear is your own inner voice, your self critic. It can work for you or against you, depending on the messages you allow.*

- Keith Harrell

# Lesson 25
# Get A Bigger Tank

Did you know that a shark grows in proportion to the size of its environment? You can completely control the size of the shark by controlling the size of the tank!

Okay, my wife just informed that this is a myth. Too bad, I'm still using it - because I want it to work for my illustration. Literary license in full use!

When I started my sales career in printing, I knew nothing about printing, a little about sales and a little more about thinking big. After 12 months of pounding my head against the proverbial sales wall, my sales were lousy, and I was deep in the hole of my draw. I decided that if I was going to be fired for lack of results it would not be for lack of effort. I resolved that my calendar would show the initiative that SHOULD produce results. Eventually, the wave of momentum caught up and the results started coming in. The big turnaround happened, when unknowingly, my boss commented across the room (not even to me) that I was tracking toward one of the top producers in the country. Before this offhand comment, my tank was the size of Central PA in terms of who I could compete with; yet, in a flash, my new tank expanded nationwide! Within about 2 years, I was the top national producer. That's right, from surviving to thriving in about 2 year's time! Now, increasing the size of my tank didn't do it alone. I needed to put in the work. As it says in the Bible, "Faith without works is dead." Do the work AND increase the tank – a great formula for success!

Don't you have a few key people in your life that, when you get around them, they make you think BIGGER? They push your boundaries and even make you squirm a bit. They believe, perhaps more than you, in what you can and should be become.

Right now, how big is your tank? Is it big enough to allow you to grow into the results you want – career, money, marriage, health? What or who defines the parameters of your tank? Your friends, your associates, your music, your words, your thoughts? Yes!

Find those people and associations that stretch your tank to fit the results you really want. Get uncomfortable, learn, grow, believe, and then put your head down and start working!

*It was character that got us out of bed, commitment that moved us into action, and discipline that enabled us to follow through.*

- Zig Ziglar

# Lesson 26
# Quality Versus Quantity

How did you learn to ride a bike? How did you learn to swing the baseball bat? How did you learn a good tennis swing? How did you become a black belt? How did you learn to swim? How did you learn to sell? You did it, adjusted accordingly, did more with more mistakes, adjusted again, and kept moving forward. Quantity precedes quality, rather than the other way around.

I read in John Maxwell's fantastic book, *Failing Forward*, a story that I will significantly paraphrase from memory. It had something to do with a class experiment involving pottery – not my secret hobby. The class was divided into two groups and each given a separate basis for grading. The first was told to produce as many bowls as they could, and they would be graded on the sheer volume (in pounds) of completed pieces. The second group was told to make one exquisite pottery bowl – their grading thus based on quality only. The next day each class offered their respective results and was graded accordingly. The class was then asked to identify what they believed to be the best quality piece from either of the two groups. Conventional wisdom would suggest this would come from the group whose focus was on quality. Of course, you've guessed that just the opposite was the case. The group focused on quantity, though having lots of poor quality pieces, did indeed have the best quality piece as well.

It truly does stand to reason that, through quantitative effort, quality can be produced. By constantly failing forward – which presumes consistent forward effort – activity allows for mistakes, adjustments and corrective change. The result – quality! A big dose of extra credit comes by having someone you trust available to direct, mentor, and coach your efforts in order to minimize the forming of poor habits and to help you adjust what you cannot see.

Whether you are looking to improve your sales skills, your relationships, your tennis swing, your driving skills, anything – do it often, learn from your mistakes and as Wilbur from Disney's *Meet the Robinson's* says, "Keep moving forward!"

*Treat people as though they were what they ought to be, and you will help them become what they are capable of becoming.*

- Johann Wolfgang von Goethe

# Lesson 27
# Leaders Treat People Into Existence

I can hear one of the most influential people in my life saying, "Mike, you'll lead far more effectively when you learn to treat people into existence." Since the rest of the world generally focuses on what people do wrong, he told me to catch people doing things right. People move to where they feel valued. Rather than seeing people where they are, we would be better to see them where they can be – which supports what they value. That may take a little faith, encouragement and forethought, but it will prove well worth it.

Have you ever heard that capacity is a state of mind? Well, it certainly is, and others can significantly influence what we believe to be that capacity. Allow me to circle back to the story in lesson 25. Years ago, while in the role of selling for a local company (and with a locally competitive mindset), my manager/owner happened to mention that I was tracking at a nationally competitive level, of which I was completely unaware. Whether he knew it or not, his passive statement elevated me from being locally competitive to seeing myself as I could be – a nationally competitive sales leader (hit that a few years later).

If you want to develop a strong team at work, at church, on the field or at home – learn the patience and perspective of seeing people beyond their current state. Remember, whether our spouse, our kids, or our team, people will generally rise to our level of expectation – especially with those who respect us most. If you want a great team, treat people into existence.

*Confidence...thrives on honesty, on honor, on the sacredness of obligations, on faithful protection and on unselfish performance. Without them it cannot live.*

- Franklin D Roosevelt

# Lesson 28
# Say What You Mean; Mean What You Say

Imagine if everyone actually said what they meant AND meant what they said – which is validated by the actions that follow. Simply put, if you promise something, follow through (mean what you say). If you want something, ask and be clear and purposeful (say what you mean). In Scripture, it says to let your "yes" mean "yes" and your "no" mean "no". No need for complicated explanation. No room for interpretation – that's what makes this so powerful! What if you had a team of people who ALWAYS said what they meant and meant what they said; their yes's were yes's and their no's were no's? How well could you predict their performance? How much could they be depended upon? How many clients, vendors, co-workers, managers, etc would love to work with them? How much time, energy, resources and ultimate leverage would that provide you? The big question is - would you make this team? Gandhi says, "Be the change you wish to see in this world" – so on a smaller level, let's agree to be the change we want to see in our team.

*Life is a 10-speed bike. Most of us have gears we have never used.*

- Charles Schulz

# Lesson 29
# Nothing Works!

In-between Success Magazine CDs, Andy Stanley POD casts and other helpful learning material, I listen to sports talk radio while I'm driving. In sports talk radio, they are constantly promoting the workout program, P90X. Well, I'm here to tell you flat out that P90X doesn't work (keep reading).

I can hear Charlie "Tremendous" Jones in his booming voice saying, "Nothing works!" He always had a way of getting our attention by starting his point backwards; though, anyone who knew him just waited for him to bring the point around. And he always did. Nothing works. Our sales plan, it doesn't work. Our business plan, it doesn't work. Our marriage, it doesn't work. Having a written sales plan, business plan or even a marriage certificate doesn't necessarily produce anything (positive) in itself. The bottom line is that we make these things work. We write a good sales plan, but then must work it with the right level of quality, attitude and consistency. We write a solid business plan, but then we make it work by proper and consistent administration, delegation and testing and measuring for effectiveness and adjustments.

Our marriage doesn't work; we work it by learning what's important to our spouse and unconditionally providing it, always pursuing, compromising and showing love and respect every day. That works because we work.

As I write this, I've been playing that little P90X DVD series daily for 10 weeks, and I can say that it does work – only because it has a committed and willing participant!

*Before a person can achieve the kind of life he wants, he must think, act, walk, talk and conduct himself in all of his affairs as would the person he wishes to become.*

-Zig Ziglar

# Lesson 30
# Get Outside Your Comfort Zone

You've all heard the story of the butterfly, the boy and the cocoon…the well intending boy helps the struggling soon-to-be butterfly to work its way out of the cocoon, and thereby seal its fate of a very short life! Without the struggle, the butterfly's wings are not saturated properly with the fluids necessary for proper growth, rendering them worthless. And everyone knows that a butterfly without wings doesn't amount to much!

Does that really apply for us, at least metaphorically? I think so. Truly, I believe that unless I get that occasional "tough" feeling in the pit of my stomach, I am probably just doing what is comfortable –sameness, rarely yields new opportunities. Seeking opportunity usually comes with facing rejection.

- Salespeople face discomfort by risking rejection when seeking opportunities to serve others.
- Business owners face discomfort and stress by risking money, time and reputation, for the possibility of reward – in terms of money, time and reputation.
- Spouses grow in their marriage by addressing difficult,

uncomfortable issues – facing conflict in the hopes of gaining understanding and relational growth.

- Kids face rejection in order to make friends – that can last a lifetime.

So let's get outside our comfort zone occasionally, if not regularly – doing things we know that are good and necessary, but maybe not easy. Like a muscle, our mental toughness is increased when challenged properly. As Robert Schuller says, "Tough times don't last, but tough people do"!

*Do not fear going forward slowly.*
*Fear only to stand still.*
- Chinese Proverb

# Lesson 31
# Three Frogs And A Decision

Three frogs were sitting on a lily pad. Two decided to jump in. How many were left? If you answered one, you may suffer from a common challenge - thinking that deciding is the end-all of commitment. Three. The answer is three. Just because two decided to jump in, doesn't mean they followed through. A decision does not a commitment make.

When making decisions, I suggest you establish a strong commitment impetus. 1). Know why you have made this decision - what is the fuel (purpose, reward) that is intended? Dwell on that reward. Brian Tracy calls this Visioning - imagining you already have what you want - seeing, touching, tasting, experiencing. Athletes do this all the time, as do successful people in all areas - sales, business, psychology, parenting, marriage, music, etc. 2). Another key impetus for growing feet to your decisions is accountability. On a formal level, find a person you respect and engage them in your accountability. Depending how you set this up and the level of involvement you need from them, make it as easy as possible for them to effectively hold you accountable. On a less formal level, you may consider "confessing" your decisions to those you do not want to let down. This can get a little tricky as you make your decisions public. I usually suggest making "go up" decisions public, and "give up" decisions private. When I decided to complete the P90X workout program last spring, I intentionally told everyone I could, not for show, but to ensure accountability. I place a high value on personal integrity and telling others adds a great deal of accountability - knowing that at any time, innocently, numerous people could check in on me. Whatever the inspiration, I completed the program 91 days after the "decision". Excellent program, by the way. Barring injury, P90X2 is likely next. Notice the lack of commitment in that sentence - "barring" and “likely" - they are both "back doors"! 3). And that leads to the last suggestion I have for this writing - speak decisive, committed words to support your good decisions. Scripture says, "Call things that are not as though they are." and "Whatsoever he saith shall also come to pass." Pretty much sums it up.

Commitment is the key. Which is more committed, the chicken or the pig? At least as far as eggs and bacon go, the pig is far more committed! I want to be the pig. No comment, please.

*Concentrate all your thoughts on the work at hand. The sun's rays do not burn until brought to a focus.*

- Alexandar Graham Bell

# Lesson 32
# Don't Confuse Enthusiasm With Priority

I was listening to a Success CD, and the speaker said something that really got my attention; he said, "Don't confuse enthusiasm with priority." As I write this, the complete context escapes me, but the point does not. If you have kids, or perhaps a dog or cat, you may remember the "Bumble Ball". This exciting, dynamic, bumbling toy would entertain the kids and the dog, sometimes until the batteries ran out. This toy is very exciting, always moving, but never really gets anywhere in particular – because it is constantly changing direction.

I know people who are much the same way – very exciting, dynamic, ever-changing, but never really getting anywhere significant (often despite clear talent and potential). There is no focus, no intention, no direction - just excitement.

If you are anything like me (and I know I am!), you've invested countless hours in "restarting" because something new or exciting (they often go together) comes along – whether it's a new book (the one I was reading wasn't that good anyway) or a new sales strategy (the old one

I started yesterday surely wasn't very good) – "new" so often looks more exciting and thereby takes priority. The Bumble Ball makes a great toy, but not a great teacher. Its enthusiasm is its priority – let's make our priorities what we are enthusiastic about.

*Be the change you wish to see in the world.*
- Mahatma Gandhi

# Lesson 33
# A Culture Is A Consistent Set Of Actions

I believe our "culture" (the attitude and actions within our environment) is often a clear reflection of ourselves. It's a mirror; what we put out comes back - eventually.

Has your company posted its values or culture list for everyone to see? Have you read it; can you recite it? Most important, do you live it and does everyone else? Just like you, I've seen lots of posted statements about vision, mission, culture, values, success traits, etc on countless office walls, web landing pages, and even bumper stickers. Woopdiddlydoo! What difference do they really make if they are not modeled – consistently? What power there is in consistency! I will even say that customers and employees often see these posted statements as disingenuous or even hypocritical – if they are not being CONSISTENTLY lived by the leaders. Now, from the perspective of that employee, he or she can "lead up" by living out those principles. That is the leader's role - so who is the leader? And is that leader consistently living out the culture they want to create and keep? Look around and what do you see? Do you see lots of drama, negativity, pessimism, blaming, and victim-mentality or do you see personal responsibility, ownership, accountability, risk-taking, innovation, and integrity? What would you prefer? Define it, and then live it – all the time.

Remember this: a culture is a consistent set of actions. Check your actions – be sure they align with your values (what you hold to be true and IMPORTANT) and that you live them CONSISTENTLY.

*Let your performance do the thinking.*
- H Jackson Brown

# Lesson 34
# You Can't Manage What You Don't Measure

When I was a kid my dad kept a ledger is his glove compartment detailing his gas mileage. After I got my license and drove HIS car I had to keep this ledger, from which he would double check his gas mileage. A good habit, I suspect, but certainly not one that mattered to me. Needless to say, my records were short of stellar, and thereby useless for real measurement. I imagine he was pretty happy when I got my own car.

Do you measure your marketing return on investment? Depending on its intent, this may be difficult. Though, in most direct marketing and some broader-scale marketing efforts, the return is measurable if only the discipline is determined and mastered. Doesn't it make sense to know if the dollars are worth the investment – at least break even? And an answer like, "Yeah, we get some hits, or sure, we've gotten a lot of calls on that ad!" doesn't cut it! How many hits and to what revenue result? How many calls, with what conversion percentage and with what ultimate yield? Knowing this information equips you for making smart future decisions.

How about us sales people? Do you know your conversion ratios? How many people/prospects do you need to see to gain a customer? If you don't do this, how do you know what activity is necessary to hit your goals? Certainly it's not always this simple, but having this information will increase your sales activity IQ in all cases.

Does this apply to outside business? Yes! How about exercise? I can still hear Tony Horton, on P90X saying "You gotta write it down! How can you know what to do, if you don't know what you did?" There's more wisdom from P90X than meets the eye! It's so true! Writing down activity sets intelligent parameters for better future decisions – like getting stronger, faster, etc.

Have you ever heard that hindsight is 20/20? Well, so is foresight, if you have good, measurable hindsight!

*It doesn't matter what you say you believe; it only matters what you do.*

- Robert Fulghum

# Lesson 35
# Are You Referable?

What is the best source for business growth – yesterday, today and tomorrow? Well, I did not pull any specific research on this, but feel pretty confident in the answer. Word of mouth is the true winner in new business development – fed mostly through service and level of experience rendered. The question is what are people saying about you, and, ultimately, are you referable?

I heard this question of "referability" while listening to a Success CD. It was an interview with Dan Kennedy, entrepreneur, speaker, author and marketing guru, who mentioned the four keys to "referability". I usually don't reference research; instead, I choose mostly to rely on life experience and common-sense, but not-so-commonly applied ideas. Though, this list is so simple and yet, so profound I had to write about it!

There is no magic bullet to being referable. And yet, even after you read these, many will go back to the norm and look for those "wow" tactics for "referability". Don't get me wrong, the "wow" can be the tipping point or differentiator – assuming you are applying these four principles consistently. So let's get these down first.

1. Be on time. A friend and highly successful entrepreneur often said, "If you can't be on time, be early." I'm usually on time, always call if not, but definitely have room for improvement here. This will go on my accountability plan immediately.
2. Finish what you start. There are many great starters out there, but few strong finishers. Finish strong, and then start something new. Be complete.
3. Follow through. Wow, how many clients have I spoken to who have need for more business, yet the leads are there. The problem is NOT following through. If you say you'll call or email or do whatever, do it; no excuses. Be predictable; boring as it sounds, people like that.
4. Say "please" and "thank you". Manners. Simple, obvious, but remarkably inconsistent in today's, hurried communication. Slow down, appreciate, and be sincerely courteous.

Common sense for sure; just not so commonly applied in today's marketplace. It's unfortunate that these can be differentiators (applied consistently).

Funny that we all learned what a world-renowned marketing genius has identified as the keys to great "referability" – in Kindergarten!

*Control your own destiny or someone else will.*

- Jack Welch

# Lesson 36
# BAM!

So, you had a great first meeting with a potential prospect – Big Whoop! Did you leave with your next meeting already scheduled? Be wary if you didn't…

BAM! Here is a proven strategy for increased sales and ultimately, and most importantly, increased service – BAM means to "book a meeting (from a meeting)". Another phrase I use to bring this point home is "close the door"! – meaning if you do not schedule a follow through/second meeting while at the first meeting, you are less likely to have a second meeting. Thus, when you leave, the "door of opportunity" is left open and can easily escape. If you maintain control – confidently and appropriately, by scheduling a follow through meeting from the first meeting - the "door of opportunity" is closed and the opportunity will not easily escape. Remember - it takes effort to cancel a meeting, but no effort to not schedule a meeting.

One mistake I still make at times is not scheduling that follow up meeting at the previous meeting, thinking that they are so excited that it will be easy to call or email and set the next meeting - only to find the fire immediately begins to let up once I leave. Consequently, "life" distracts my prospect from the benefit we once mutually raved about. Imagine blowing up a balloon and not tying it – the air (opportunity, value, benefit, excitement) flows out immediately. Make sense?

Also remember - if you serve your prospect appropriately by diligently and sincerely learning about them, their role, challenges, opportunities, etc., and find a pathway to serve them (with mutual agreement), you are now the expert or consultant and you owe it to your future client to guide the process.

Keep in mind that this is a skill – its application is not always appropriate, but likely applies within the 80/20 rule – a great habit to apply at least 80% of the time.

Trust that you'll know the difference. And when you're in that next meeting, don't forget to "close the door" on your way out.

*"Nothing in the world can take the place of persistence. Talent will not; nothing is more common than unsuccessful men with talent. Genius will not; unrewarded genius is almost a proverb. Education will not; the world is full of educated derelicts. Persistence and determination alone are omnipotent."*

- Calvin Coolidge

# Lesson 37
# The Definition of Selling

Several months back, I had an opportunity to meet with an individual about a potential project. Though he was not offering the opportunity exclusively to me, I was the one in his office at the time, meaning I was in a strong closing position. As we discussed what he really needed, it became apparent to me that, though I felt I could serve him, I knew of someone else who was better positioned for the specific type of project he had in mind. Rather than offer myself as the solution provider, even though that is the basis upon which he reached out to me, I referred him to what I felt was a better solution. He met with the individual I recommended, and they moved forward with the project. I did not walk away with the sale, but did I sell him? My litmus test is this – did I lead him to a decision that was good for him? Yes. Then I sold him.

Zig Ziglar defined sales as "transference of conviction or feeling". Strategic Coach, Dan Sullivan defines sales this way, "Selling is getting someone intellectually engaged in a future result that is good for them and getting them to emotionally commit to take action to achieve that result".

My personal definition for sales is this: "Leading people to decisions that are good for them".

As illustrated in the true story above, I may "sell you" without you buying my product or service. In accepting my "sale" you will, however, take my advice – which may be to not buy, to buy elsewhere, or to buy differently.

You see, most people see a sale as *me* selling *you* to buy from *me*. Thankfully this is not the case - because that is a lot of pressure! The only pressure I have felt in "selling" since starting my coaching and training company has been to serve the person I am communicating with. I feel no pressure to get you to buy, but a lot of pressure to lead you to make a decision that is good for you. I do this by taking on the responsibility to learn about you, your situation, your needs and wants and your interests (through great questions) and then providing a professionally credible set of solutions.

That type of pressure I can handle and even look forward to!

*"The ultimate measure of a man is not where he stands in moments of comfort and convenience, but where he stands in times of controversy".*

\- Martin Luther King, Jr.

# Lesson 38
# Sales - Three Critical Behaviors

For nearly 25 years I've been in the sales world, including training and coaching many individuals and teams along the way. Through all of this, I believe that ultimate success or failure comes down to three critical behaviors. Most everything else falls within these three or have far less overall impact. So if you are not selling as much as you would like, or if you are, but you're giving away your life and profits to do it, evaluate your results on these three points:

- **Activity** – Are you "worthy" of the results you desire based on what you schedule in your calendar - # calls, # appointments, etc? Do you "touch" enough real opportunities, open enough doors, see enough people, and reach out enough times? In terms of new business activity, are you sitting still, warming up, jogging, running or sprinting?
- **Quality** (skill) – As you increase your activity level, are you working your processes with quality and skill? Are you communicating well - asking good questions and actively listening? Are you asking for

the work, for testimonials, for referrals? Do you know how to do these things? Have you scripted any of your processes? How well do you know your industry, product and competition?

- **Attitude** (mindset) – John Maxwell calls this the "difference maker". What are you thinking when you pick up that phone, knock on that door or ask for the order? Do you expect to succeed or expect to fail? Are you the apologetic salesperson whose voice tone rises when asking for a commitment? Do you believe in yourself, your company, your product or service? Do you feed your mind with the attitudes, ideals and success you want to reap?

Now, this isn't likely new for anyone – we all inherently know these things. But do we? To know and not to do is not to know. The challenge is that common sense is often not consistently applied. Pay attention to, and ultimately address, these three areas, and you'll begin to see tremendous results. By the way, if you are asking which to focus on first, I suggest activity. Why? It's a whole lot easier to steer a car once it's moving!

*Procrastination is opportunity's natural assassin.*

- Victor Kiam

# Lesson 39
# Tie Up Loose Ends!

Messy hair, shoes untied, shirt-tail hanging out – not judging here, but not likely a person of efficiency and focus. Fortunately, I had my hair cut a few days ago, no way you'll catch me with my shirt-tail hanging out, and I stopped NOT tying my shoes on purpose around the age of 16 (maybe that was the 80's version of "pants on the ground") – I'll definitely take the untied shoes!

The point is - I don't like lose ends! They mess me up. Look bad? Yes; but more importantly they trip me up throughout my day. I'm not really talking priority stuff here – like time with my wife, my kids, sales calls, key project preparation or things that have the greatest impact on my present and future. I'm talking about the nagging things that muddy up my focus and energy while I take on the priorities. Imagine walking the dog with your shoe laces untied. It won't keep you from finishing the walk and it won't likely slow you down much, but does it bother you? – Likely, and under the right (or wrong) circumstances, it can really trip you up!

I had a file on my desk for two months about calling

a service provider. A call that was not critical, but necessary; not urgent, but upon completion, would really be helpful. It sat there every day, disciplined, whispering gently to me... "I am here, not a big deal/not a priority, but a nasty little thorn in your side. And, I'll be here again tomorrow, as the pain doesn't seem to be enough for you to deal with me." Anyone relating? Soon, I had another administrative issue come up that found its way on top of the other file – on my desk, whispering ever so loudly like the other!

Eventually, I got tired of it, pulled up Outlook and scheduled an hour the following week to deal with these two issues (by then it was four!). Immediately, the whispering stopped. A week later, I made the calls and 15 minutes later, the files were cleared! But what of the two months those issues quietly haunted my "disciplined, productive nature"? They were with me the whole time, like a shirt tail hanging out, slightly bothering me, slightly sapping energy, slightly effecting my attitude, slightly owning a piece of my day, and all along, completely unnecessary!

So - tie up loose ends – immediately if appropriate. If not, schedule it and be done with it – until the scheduled time comes. Then, focus and get it done, completely.

I don't like untied shoe laces. So, now I double knot. That's part of the will to prepare to win – another topic for another day. And, if they come untied, I tie them, right away and walk on, happy.

*It's not enough to be busy. So are the ants. The question is what are we busy about?*

- Henry David Thoreau

# Lesson 40
# Are You Busy Or Productive?

How many times do you get through the day or week feeling like you were incredibly busy – always working, trudging through the never-ending task list, retrieving and making calls, emails, texts, tweets and more – but not accomplishing anywhere near what you expected? So much of society seems to equate a busy person with a successful one. The ultimate question at the end of the day is whether or not you've moved closer to reaching your goal. Were you busy or productive? But knowing this is nebulous without clearly defined goals or benchmarks upon which progress can be measured. Even deeper is defining the goals in such a way that they are suitable benchmarks on the pathway to achieving your ultimate vision. A mentor once told me that efficiency is doing the job right, while effectiveness is doing the right job right.

So, before you engage in another busy week, consider planning ahead to ensure what you will be doing is a productive part ("the right job") in reaching your goal. If it isn't, delegate or drop it; and if you feel you must do it, prioritize it to be done only after your most productive tasks have been completed. This way, whether busy or not, you will be productive. As Todd Duncan says in his book, *High Trust Selling*, "Sometimes you have to slow down to speed up".

*Productivity is never an accident. It is always the result of the commitment to excellence, intellect, planning and focused effort.*

- Paul J Meyer

# Lesson 41
# Systematic Success

What one word comes to mind when I say "system"? The word that comes to my mind is "leverage". An effective system provides leverage, allowing greater results with less effort over time. How easy is it to drive to work each morning? How stressed are you in the journey, wondering where to turn, thinking through how to most effectively arrive on time, and how to navigate the various traffic signals along the way? I suspect very little. You don't have to re-think it each time; you just go. That is how it can be when we develop a system. Specifically, in terms of selling, what is your system? What system does your company endorse? This is not to take away from originality, and in fact, it can provide greater freedom for it. If you limit the thinking necessary to do what has already been leveraged, you open yourself up to be more creative within the process. An effective sales system should leverage your energy, resources and money – allowing you to accomplish more with less, while providing a proven pathway for others to follow.

So go on – create the steps; create the tools and templates for each step; build any key scripts; then define specific skills, processes and objectives for each step and ultimately to use in effectively moving through the system. Execute, evaluate and adjust.

*As you walk down the fairway of life you must smell the roses, for you only get to play one round.*

- Ben Hogan

# Lesson 42

# Downtime Leads To Better Uptime

In lesson 12, I wrote about sharpening the axe. No matter how well you swing, or how many times you swing, there is a law of diminishing return as the axe becomes dull. The same is true for you and me. It's not about the amount of hours we devote to our professions, the time we put in at the gym, the number of books we read, or even how much time we spend with those we love (though quantity time does pay big dividends with family!). Ultimately it's about the presence, focus and energy we devote in all these areas. Fatigue and stress kill quality and become self defeating.

So what do you do to recharge those Rhinoceros batteries? Here are some ideas that may help:

- Get some sleep –
    - People need between 7.5 and 8 hours of sleep for optimal health and mental clarity - *Success Magazine*, June 2011.
    - Our bodies burn 30% less calories when sleep deprived – *Brain Rules*, by Dr. John Medina

- Go on vacation – Delegate to your team and trust them; get away with your family - with only one major responsibility – enjoying the moments and building the memories
- Enjoy a weekend getaway – Especially if you are married!
- Get outside – Get some fresh air – Go on a hike, walk or bike ride. It's amazing how energizing the outdoors can be (but don't bring your cell phone!)
- Exercise – Consistently shown to REDUCE fatigue and BOOST energy levels; take time to exercise and you'll need LESS time to be MORE productive and FEEL a whole lot better overall!

Lastly, choose to enjoy the journey and not just focus on the destination. As I look back on my life, it seems the real rewards are found more in the journey anyway. Let's not wish away the days just to get to the weekend; rather, let's choose to enjoy the moments. These are the moments that make up most of our lives anyway – make them count.

So let's make time for downtime – and you may find it becomes your real uptime.

*A really great talent finds its happiness in execution.*

- Johann Wolfgang von Goethe

# Lesson 43
# Get Your FACTs Straight

A recent web search on New Year's Resolutions showed that 45% of Americans usually make New Year's Resolutions, but only 8% actually achieve them. Resolutions usually fall into categories of money, health, relationships, and education/self improvement.

Here are a few questions to consider: If you are in sales, how effective is your activity? If you are in marketing, what kind of results are you getting and does it cover your break even? Is that advertisement really paying for itself or would the money and time investment be better leveraged elsewhere? If you are striving for better health, are you aware of your consistency and the measure of your results?

Many of us don't know the answers to these questions. Have you ever considered the value of testing and measuring to be sure your plan is working? This, of course, assumes you have formulated a plan in the first place!

It's time to get your FACTs straight. FACT stands for Formulate, Act, Compare and Tune. Whether sales, marketing, human resources, strategy planning, or even exercise – take the proper time to formulate a plan for your desired outcomes, then act upon your strategy. Here is where I see most failure occur – people simply don't do what they say they'll do. They just don't ACT – at least not consistently and not long enough to gain a true measure of value. Once a proper amount of time has passed with consistent execution, compare your outcomes with your plans - measure the results. Finally, it's time for tuning. This is all about making proper adjustments – execute better, scrap it, change it, adjust the goal –whatever it takes to be sure you're always working toward an effective, measurable result.

There you have it – FACT. To move ahead and be sure you're further this year than you are today, it's time to get your FACTs straight!

*The main thing is to keep the main thing the main thing.*

- Steven Covey

# Lesson 44
# The Main Thing

Single minded focus can be absolutely liberating as it relates to getting results. Ever play baseball with gnats flying all around you? Ever run in the soft sand or deep snow? Ever try to have a conversation with your wife while watching football (danger alert!)? Focus is critical in all things important. What this means for me is that when it comes to the important actions of my day, multi-tasking is out the window. Multi-tasking has its place (somewhere, I guess), but in order to truly gain momentum and leverage the "zone state" that yields the best results, single-minded focus is the way to go. Consider this illustration: take a magnifying glass outside on a warm, sunny day and hold it over some dry grass (or a small insect if you're a 7 year old boy!) for 1 or 2 minutes and what happens? The light is focused into heat and starts burning its subject! Yet, you could walk around all day with that magnifying glass, with constant sunlight passing through, never focusing it in any one place and how much heat is generated? None. Use this principal by truly being present for the things that are most important at a particular time – in other words, determine the main thing, and then keep the main thing the main thing.

*Patience is the companion of wisdom.*
- Saint Augustine

# Lesson 45
# A Sustainable Pace

North Point Ministries (Andy Stanley) posted a podcast called the "Rest App". You'll have to listen to the podcast to fully appreciate the context, but here is the question posed that resonated with me: "Are you moving at a sustainable pace?" Good question – but the answer is tricky, as it becomes alarmingly clear only when viewed from a distance. Are you running too fast? Are you hitting your work so hard that other parts of your life are suffering? Perhaps, it's not the work, but something else that you're chasing too hard, too fast? Do you often feel rushed? Are you thinking about too many things when you should be more "present"? Do you believe that the longer and harder you work the better off you are? Here's a big one: Are you sleeping at least 7 hours a day? I've heard studies that indicate less than 7 hours of sleep a day can cost the average adult 10-12 years of life on the back end. Yikes!

This is not to debate the validity of working hard, who can live well on less sleep, or "seasonal" times when the increased pace is inevitable. I simply want to explore what I have often heard, and innately known is true –

sometimes we simply need to slow down in order to truly speed up. Knowing this is predicated on knowing the things that matter most in our lives. In fact, when taking the 10,000 foot view, things like our faith, health, family and friends are truly what matter most. Slowing down simply allows us to enjoy and appreciate what matters most. Slowing down may even improve our productivity - by sharpening our focus, increasing our energy and re-charging our passion. As Jeff Henderson, the Podcast speaker says, "You'll move to a better place, when you move at a sustainable pace".

*Our doubts are traitors that make us lose the good we might oft win by fearing to attempt.*

- Mark Twain

# Lesson 46

# The Comfort of Change

If change is comfortable, you're doing it wrong.

My son Mitchell is a tennis player. He loves it. He's also extremely coachable, as long as it's not his dad doing the coaching. Truth be told, the best coaching at this point comes from him to me anyway.

Over the past few weeks he's been helping me with my serve – working on grip, position, feet, movement, ball toss, and leverage – just a few little things to consider ALL AT ONCE! When we really started adjusting my serve, the grip he showed me was awkward, and I complained in my best subtle fashion. You know how to do it, too – you complain with a smile– that way it seems like you're kidding, yet you've managed to get it on record that you don't like it! Well, when I offered up my subtle whining, he provided some pretty good advice. This 14 year old profoundly said to me, "Dad, if the change is comfortable, then you're doing it wrong."

Wow! That hit home, though I can't say I haven't been silently arguing over the past few weeks. I'm 47. Why do I care about the "perfect" serve anyway? Here's why I care

- if for no other reason, submitting to proper teaching is a much better example for my son!

Regardless of my personal struggle with change on the tennis court, the advice is dead on accurate. How much change do we take on, only to adjust it to a more "comfortable" level? When we do this, we rob ourselves of the real rewards that come from correct and consistent change.

Do you want a better tennis game? How about a raise? Do you want a better, more rewarding career? Do you want a better marriage, a better relationship with key people in your lives?

Change. Don't adjust to your level of comfort; keep it consistent with proper coaching and the ultimate reward you want.

By the way, my serve is starting to improve. Major headway on the court yesterday. Thanks, buddy.

*To do two things at once is to do neither.*
- Publius Syrus

# Lesson 47
# The Person Who Is Everywhere Is Nowhere

If you give a mouse a cookie, he'll ask for a glass of milk; when you give him the milk, he'll probably ask for a straw; when he's finished, he'll ask for a napkin…and so on, and so on. Ever been the mouse? Ever had multiple tasks to complete – begin one, then part way through go to another that is slightly related or connected, then take on an extension of that one, only to forget the first task! Not much gets done (well). Here is a statement I heard years ago that has stuck with me and often gets broadcast in my mind at just the right time – "the person who is everywhere is nowhere".

Now, some of you reading this are masters at effective multi-tasking (that may be debatable), but most of us could benefit from a little restraint and focus when it comes to what's important. Just remember the next time you are "listening" to one of your kids' stories AND writing an email, organizing some bills, or even watching a show or the game – the person who is everywhere is nowhere. Trying to be too many places at once means that all those places suffer by not having all of me "present" – and for me, that would mean not really being there for my son or daughter (wife, mother, client, etc.) - and that is simply not acceptable! Perhaps there are exceptions, but when it comes to the big rocks – I've found the sharpshooter approach generally is far more worthwhile and rewarding than the shotgun approach (metaphor only!).

So when it comes to your employee, your manager, your wife, your son, your client, or whatever you are doing that is truly important – honor them by not trying to be everywhere else.

*If you chase two rabbits, both will escape.*

- Anonymous

# Lesson 48
# Are You Distracted By Shiny, New Objects?

Do you remember the movie UP and the dog named Doug? What a great name! You may remember that Doug and the others dogs were easily distracted when it came to squirrels.

My squirrel is anything "new" – new books, new exercise plans, a new sales plan, new whatever. This does not apply in the case of my wife! She's always new to me anyway.

But I must admit, especially in terms of professional and physical improvement and discipline, I used to be consistently tripped up by the squirrel of "newness". New always seemed better – I guess because it was, well, NEW! It looked better, smelled better and just seemed like a better way. This was especially true when compared to the boring, stale, plan I had been working so diligently for 2 or 3 solid weeks!

The problem is that, while new can be better (though it often is NOT), better isn't the issue; consistency is. Think about it. Even if the new idea is a better one, how long will you apply it before the next new one comes along?

It's like getting city mileage when you can be and should be getting highway mileage.

Do you change your sales plan or approach too quickly, because you learn of a new one and new seems better? Do you change your workout plan too quickly because you learn about a new one and new seems better? Do you have a bunch of unfinished books because new seems better? I encourage you – when it comes to your sales efforts, in particular, give your plans time to develop and truly provide enough feedback to determine if change is truly justified. Don't stay in a stale, stagnating, and boring plan, but don't change just for the sake of change either.

Effecting change is not an event; it is a process – and thereby takes consistent and intentional effort in order to become entrenched into the culture of an individual, team and/or company.

*One of the greatest gifts you can give someone is the gift of attention.*

- Jim Rohn

# Lesson 49
# Listening Makes You Smarter

"You're not listening to me!" – One of the worst, yet most valuable sales lessons I've ever experienced. I was in a sales call when the prospect made this very accurate assessment of me. He was absolutely right as I spent most of my time thinking of what to ask and how to stay on track, missing all the cues he was giving me - all the education I had to learn from what he was saying. So worried I would miss something important in the sales process, I missed the most important part – what mattered to him!

I've heard it said that listening makes you smarter. Does listening really affect IQ? – not likely; but then again, what difference does IQ have on our ability to develop and grow relationships? In this sense, "smarter" is about listening to the point of knowing what questions to ask – because people tell us! Learn all about this in Allan Pease's short, but powerful book called *Questions are the Answers.* Questions lead to answers that in turn develop into smarter, deeper, more relating questions. While hearing is passive, listening is the active part that happens after you have asked a question. This is where you apply their answers to your next questions. Want to get to know someone? Ask questions, listen, ask more, and listen more. Truly, most people will keep providing fuel for you to keep that conversation going, making you far more interesting and attractive than the passive listener.

According to Jim Rohn, "One of the greatest gifts you can give someone is the gift of attention." Very few would disagree with the value of truly giving someone your full attention. My wife has often said, "People move to where they feel valued." Think about that. Your kids, your spouse, your friends, your co-workers, your prospects and your team – they all move to where they feel valued. Are they moving toward you?

*People don't care how much you know until they know how much you care.*

- Theodore Roosevelt

# Lesson 50
# Prescription Before Diagnosis Is Malpractice

Recently I heard someone say that sales people often show up and throw up! Not a good impression, for sure! These salespeople are guilty of offering solutions to problems they don't know exist - they're telling, not selling. The good news is that if you are not that person, you're competition might be – which makes your job a lot easier! Keep in mind, this isn't just a sales thing; if what you do involves any form of persuasive communication, asking good questions is critical to your success – and theirs. Challenge yourself in your next meeting to get the other person talking twice as much as you do. This can be difficult with certain personalities, but if you strive for it, you'll learn the best way to get the other person talking is to keep asking (worthy) questions.

Questions also help you maintain control. Think about it – if someone asks you a question, protocol says you answer, and then they ask, you answer, and so on. The way to take that control back is to answer their question with a question. They ask a question, you answer and ask one back, and now you're back in control!

Questions make you (seem) smarter. Questions show you're interested. Questions demonstrate your professionalism. Questions guide the conversation. Questions lead to meaningful discussion. Questions take patience. Questions fuel curiosity. Questions show you care. Questions are the answers!

*No man becomes rich unless he enriches others.*

- Andrew Carnegie

# Lesson 51

## Are You Working IN Your Relationships Or ON Your Relationships?

Have you read the best seller by Michael Gerber, *E-Myth*? You may remember the big question, "Are you working ON your business or IN your business?" The truth is that most business owners spend far too much time doing their business, rather than investing time working on their business – strategy, planning, training, recruiting, systems improvements, etc.

All that said, it occurred to me that this similar principle applies to our relationships as well. Parenting, marriage, friendships, and even client/customer relationships can, and often do, become very reactive – simply doing the relationship, responding to requests, paying household bills, being "side by side" with the TV on, working two separate careers, often passing in the night. Nothing innately wrong with these things, but I'd like to suggest investing more time ON the relationship – rather than working IN it. For clients this may involve a client loyalty plan – finding ways to proactively serve and build value in the relationship. These are the things you do for them when they don't necessarily need anything – a client appreciation event, a lunch get-together, an article of personal interest to them, connecting them to people you know and believe they would appreciate knowing. For marriage and parenting, it may be creative date nights – with your spouse, and yes, even with your kids. Imagine taking your daughter out to lunch or a movie, just because. How about reading and learning from others through books, videos, church or other events? How about a family night, where each kid and adult gets a turn at choosing what to do as a family on certain nights? How about hiking? Anything to promote meaningful conversation, laughter, or any positive connection, certainly pays huge short and long term dividends.

I've read that fathers spend minutes a day at best communicating positively with their kids. I don't know if that's true, but I can see how it happens. Let's go back to Covey's story of the rocks in the jar, identify the rocks and become deliberate about putting those rocks in our jar first. I'm in.

*Every man dies. Not every man lives. The only limits to the possibilities in your life tomorrow are the 'buts' you use today.*

- Les Brown

# Lesson 52
# Words To Lose By

In 1982 I ran the Philadelphia marathon. It was a goal set for many reasons. Both reasons were a bit prideful, but not really all bad. First, none of my teammates on the x country team had run one and since I was not the top runner, this would be my personal claim to fame! Also, and maybe more important…my dad had run more than 60 marathons, and I felt being qualified as a son required at least one marathon! I only boast about one marathon and that was 29 years ago. One attempt, one personal victory – and a lot of it had to do with choosing the right language.

Here is the key: When I started the race, I was not thinking "if" I finish; I was thinking "when" I finish. I did not set out to "try"; I set out to "do". And I didn't even consciously understand the difference in those words. Yoda did not cross my mind saying, "There is no try, only do!" John Maxwell says, "Losers focus on what they are going through; winners focus on what they are going to". I believe he is referencing attitudes rather than people. I knew I had to complete one marathon and the best way to get that done without trying over and over (a painful proposition!) was to focus on what I was going to. This was best accomplished with the right language up front. By saying "when" I finish, I eliminated having to "try" again! Once and done. Goal accomplished!

Words mean things. "When" and "do" are words of commitment, action and confidence. "If" and "try" are words that lack commitment, intensity, and follow through. They leave a back door, a plan B – and when plan A is what you really want, having a plan B may be one too many options.

If says "I might"; when says "I will." Try is about deciding; do is about executing. So, moving forward, and as much as possible, replace your "if" and "try" with "when" and "do". When you do, life will pay out big time!

# About the Author

**Mike is the owner of IntegrityWorks Coaching** – An integrity-driven training company focused on professional speaking and training in the areas of motivation, communication, performance, teamwork, relationships, leadership, sales development and sales management. Additional one on one coaching provides direct personal and professional development through sales, executive and life coaching.

For over 20 years, Mike has been an exceptional sales and business leader with proven experience in professional speaking, one on one coaching and development, sales planning and execution, and training and workshop facilitation, while building strong and lasting relationships with clients, associates and partners.

Mike and his wife Amy have been married for over 23 years – committed to an exciting relationship centered in their faith and what Amy calls CPR (compromise, pursuit, and respect). Mike and Amy have three children – their first three protégés in life and plan nearly everything around family.

Integrity Works coaching

## Have Mike speak at your next event!

Mike is available for keynote presentations and workshops on topics including, but not limited to, attitude and motivation, sales, sales management, leadership, communication, time management, teambuilding and goal achievement. For more information or to schedule Mike as a presenter, please call 717-226-4306 or email sales@integrityworkscoaching.com. You can also learn more by visiting www.integrityworkscoaching.com.